# LAOS
## in Pictures

**Matt Doeden**

**Twenty-First Century Books**

# Contents

Lerner Publishing Group realizes that current information and statistics quickly become out of date. To extend the usefulness of the Visual Geography Series, we developed www.vgsbooks.com, a website offering links to up-to-date information, as well as in-depth material, on a wide variety of subjects. All of the websites listed on www.vgsbooks.com have been carefully selected by researchers at Lerner Publishing Group. However, Lerner Publishing Group is not responsible for the accuracy or suitability of the material on any website other than www.lernerbooks.com. It is recommended that students using the Internet be supervised by a parent or teacher. Links on www.vgsbooks.com will be regularly reviewed and updated as needed.

Website address: www.lernerbooks.com

Twenty-First Century Books
A division of Lerner Publishing Group
241 First Avenue North
Minneapolis, MN 55401 U.S.A.

web enhanced @ w w w . v g s b o o k s . c o m

## CULTURAL LIFE 46

▶ Religion. Festivals, Literature, and the Arts. Crafts. Music and Dance. Sports and Recreation. Food.

## THE ECONOMY 56

▶ Agriculture and Forestry. Manufacturing and Mining. Services and Tourism. Transportation and Communication. Energy. The Future.

## FOR MORE INFORMATION

Library of Congress Cataloging-in-Publication Data

Doeden, Matt.
    Laos in pictures / by Matt Doeden. — Rev. and expanded.
      p.   cm. — (Visual geography series)
    Includes bibliographical references and index.
    ISBN-13: 978-0-8225-6590-1 (lib. bdg. : alk. paper)
    ISBN-10: 0-8225-6590-0 (lib. bdg. : alk. paper)
    1. Laos—Juvenile literature. 2. Laos—Pictorial works—Juvenile literature. I. Title. II. Series
DS555.3.D64 2007
959.4—dc22                                          2006018880

Manufactured in the United States of America
1 2 3 4 5 6 - BP - 12 11 10 09 08 07

# INTRODUCTION

With a population of 6.2 million, Laos is the most thinly settled nation in Southeast Asia. Mountainous, with no access to oceans, the nation is isolated by geography as well as by the policies of its government. Even within its borders, many of Laos's people have little contact with one another. Some populations are virtually untouched by the modern world.

Although people have lived in Laos for thousands of years, the country's recorded past begins in the fourteenth century A.D. Historians believe the first inhabitants of the area lived in the highlands of northern Laos.

Later settlers came from China by following the Mekong River. This waterway runs south from China through Laos, Cambodia, and Vietnam. Early Laotians farmed and hunted along the river. For centuries traders and immigrants arrived in the region from India and China. They introduced new political systems and religious faiths. As these newcomers intermarried with the original inhabitants of Laos, a distinct Laotian nation emerged.

The first Laotian states were small kingdoms. They arose in the four-teenth century and ruled central Laos from the historic capital of Louangphrabang. Despite occasional problems, these realms lasted for several hundred years.

Internal conflicts erupted at the start of the 1700s. Different members of the Laotian royal family sought support from their powerful neighbors in Burma (present-day Myanmar), Siam (modern Thailand), and Vietnam. These foreign governments divided and ruled Laos until the late nineteenth century. At that time, French explorers began moving up the Mekong River into Laos. By 1893 France was claiming much of Southeast Asia—including Laos, Cambodia, and Vietnam—as its colony. Collectively, these countries became known as French Indochina.

During World War II (1939–1945), the Japanese swept across lower Asia and took control of French Indochina. After the defeat of Japan in 1945, an independence movement strengthened in the Laotian countryside. Members of the Lao royal family rallied the

CHINA

MYANMAR
(BURMA)

Mekong River

Ban Muang

Nam Ou

Nam Tha

Louangphrabang

Nam Khan

Mekong River

Nam Ngum

VIETNAM

Nam Ngum
Reservoir

Nam Ngum
Dam

Vientiane

Mittaphab Bridge

Nam
Theun

Gulf of
Tonkin

Mekong River

THAILAND

Savannakhet

Ban Sung

Pakxe

Pakxe

Champasak

Mekong
River

CAMBODIA

CHINA

MYANMAR
(BURMA)

INDIA

LAOS

South
China Sea

PACIFIC
OCEAN

INDONESIA

INDIAN
OCEAN

AUSTRALIA

1000 Miles
1000 KM

## Laos

— International border
— Ho Chi Minh Trail
⊛ Capital city
• City
⋈ Bridge
– Dam

0          100 Miles

0          100 KM

N

Laotians against French control. In 1953 France agreed to grant Laos its independence.

But turmoil among Laos's many political groups worsened. One group, the royalists, supported a monarchy. Another favored a Communist government, in which the state would control and own all industries, factories, and businesses.

After France granted independence to Laos and the rest of French Indochina, power struggles brought warfare to much of Southeast Asia. During the 1960s, civil war broke out in Laos between the Pathet Lao, a Communist group, and anti-Communist opposition. At the same time, the people of neighboring Vietnam and Cambodia fought in similar struggles. In 1975 Pathet Lao forces captured the modern capital of Vientiane. They formed a government that outlawed opposing political parties.

At least 350,000 citizens have fled Laos since the Communist takeover. These people left their homeland to escape a system that denies most personal freedoms, including the rights to privacy, free speech, assembly, and travel in and out of the country.

The policies of the Pathet Lao regime led to economic decline in the 1980s. Laotian leaders adopted several important reforms to address the problems. By the 1990s, Laos was permitting new shops to open and allowing farmers to sell their goods privately. By the early 2000s, the nation was beginning to join the world economy. Although Laos has made changes in economic policy, political and social reforms are progressing much more slowly.

The country has maintained its single-party political system in which opposition parties are illegal. Laos also remains overwhelmingly poor, and its citizens have little freedom to improve their situation. Whether a better life awaits the people of Laos remains to be seen as the nation continues to face an uncertain future.

# THE LAND

Laos is the only landlocked country (surrounded entirely by land) in Southeast Asia. It lies in the middle of the Indochinese Peninsula—a long, narrow landform that also includes Vietnam, Cambodia, Thailand, and Myanmar. With a total land area of 91,430 square miles (236,800 square kilometers), Laos is slightly smaller than the state of Oregon.

China borders Laos on the north. Vietnam is to the east of Laos, while Cambodia is on the south. Thailand lies west of Laos, and Myanmar sits to the northwest. Laos extends about 650 miles (1,047 km) in length from the northwest to the southeast. The nation's widest point, in the north, is 290 miles (467 km) from west to east. By contrast, parts of the southeastern panhandle—the thin, armlike projection of land that makes up the middle of the country—do not reach 100 miles (161 km) in width.

 ## Topography

Laos is mainly a mountainous nation, without much level land. This makes communication, transportation, and farming difficult. It also

contributes to the Laotian people's isolation from one another and from the rest of Southeast Asia. The mountains of the northeast cover more than two-thirds of the country. Narrow valleys that hold dense rain forests separate the mountains. Plateaus (flat highlands) in the north are among the nation's few flat areas, along with the Mekong floodplains of the southwest.

More than 90 percent of the Laotian land rises at least 600 feet (183 meters) above sea level. Mount Phou Bia in north central Laos is the country's highest point at 9,248 feet (2,819 m) above sea level. Its lowest point is 230 feet (70 m), along the Mekong River.

Laos has four main geographic regions: the Annamese Cordillera, the Tran Ninh Plateau, the Cammon Plateau, and the Bolovens Plateau. Along the eastern border with Vietnam are the rugged peaks of the Annamese Cordillera. At the narrowest point of the Laotian panhandle, these mountains reach the valley of the Mekong River. This waterway forms much of Laos's western border. Limestone caves are common at the

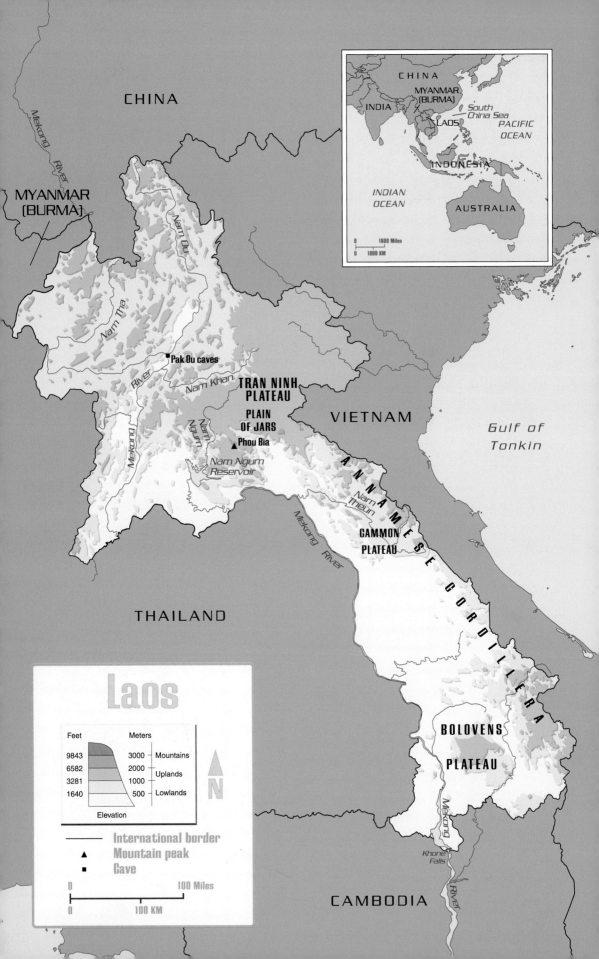

CHINA

MYANMAR
(BURMA)

*Mekong River*

*Nam Ou*

*Nam Tha*

■ Pak Ou caves

*Nam Khan*

TRAN NINH
PLATEAU

*Nam Ngum*

PLAIN
OF JARS

▲ Phou Bia

Nam Ngum
Reservoir

*Mekong River*

VIETNAM

Gulf of
Tonkin

*Nam Theun*

CAMMON
PLATEAU

A N N A M E S E   C O R D I L L E R A

THAILAND

BOLOVENS

PLATEAU

*Mekong River*

Khone
Falls

CAMBODIA

CHINA

MYANMAR
(BURMA)

INDIA

South
China Sea

PACIFIC
OCEAN

LAOS

INDONESIA

INDIAN
OCEAN

AUSTRALIA

0        1000 Miles

0        1000 KM

## Laos

| Feet | Meters | |
|---|---|---|
| 9843 | 3000 | Mountains |
| 6582 | 2000 | Uplands |
| 3281 | 1000 | |
| 1640 | 500 | Lowlands |

Elevation

N

——— International border

▲ Mountain peak

■ Cave

0        100 Miles

0        100 KM

southern end of the Annamese chain. A series of three plateaus runs north to south through the center of the country. The northernmost plateau is the Tran Ninh Plateau, which includes a grassland known as the Plain of Jars. This grassland takes its name from the large ancient containers found there. In central Laos, the Cammon Plateau reaches the foothills of the Annamese Cordillera. This plateau has karst—limestone formations including sinkholes, underground streams, and caverns. At the southern end of Laos, near the border with Cambodia, is the Bolovens Plateau. Steep slopes surround this fertile, wooded plain.

The floodplains of the Mekong River are Laos's only other flatlands. In these regions, seasonal flooding

## PLAIN OF JARS

Mysterious stone jars are scattered throughout Laos's Plain of Jars. Made mostly of sandstone and granite, the jars weigh up to 13 tons (12 metric tons). They range from 3 to 10 feet (1 to 3 m) tall. The original purpose of the jars is a mystery. Archaeologists believe that early Laotians may have used them 1,500 to 2,000 years ago as funeral urns or for food storage. In some places, clusters of jars form a straight path that archaeologists believe may have once indicated a trade route from northern India.

**Jars on Laos's Plain of Jars** are 3 to 10 feet (1 to 3 m) tall.

leaves rich silt (soil) deposits. Heavily farmed, these lowlands boast the many irrigated rice paddies that provide much of the nation's food supply.

## Rivers

The Mekong River is the main waterway of Southeast Asia. It flows for 2,600 miles (4,186 km) from its source in the mountains of Tibet. From this remote area to the north of Laos, the river churns between steep mountainsides. It then passes through the Golden Triangle—the region where Laos, Myanmar, and Thailand meet. The Mekong forms much of Laos's western border before exiting the country at Khone Falls, 1,200 miles (1,932 km) to the southeast. The river travels into Cambodia and then into the Mekong Delta of southern Vietnam. There it empties into the South China Sea, an arm of the Pacific Ocean.

In **a rice paddy near Vientiane,** a woman reaches out to catch a fish in her bamboo basket. Floodwaters from the Mekong River irrigate many rice paddies in the area.

A tropical sun sets on the tranquil **Mekong River near Louangphrabang.**

Large rocks make travel on the upper Mekong dangerous. Travel is most difficult during the dry season, when the river's water level is low. In the rainy summer months, the Mekong can swell to 40 feet (12 m) above its banks. It can extend to 14 miles (23 km) in width. Steep falls and strong rapids obstruct the passage of river craft during this season.

In certain seasons and in certain areas, the river provides Laotians with a useful transportation route. Riverboats carry crops and livestock to market and people from town to town. The Mekong also deposits hundreds of tons of fertile soil on the farmland and rice paddies of western Laos. In addition, the river supplies fish for lowland dwellers.

Other important rivers in Laos include the Nam Ou, the Nam Tha, and the Nam Ngum. All of these waterways run westward into the Mekong River. The Nam Ngum powers a large hydroelectric power station near Vientiane, Laos's capital city.

Most Laotian waterways empty into the Mekong. But a few northern rivers flow eastward through Vietnam. Many of these small rivers feed Laotian rice paddies, allowing some growers to raise two crops each year. The rivers empty into the Gulf of Tonkin, another arm of the South China Sea.

**Monsoon rains flooded rural Ban Sung** in the early 2000s. Residents carefully crossed floodwaters on a plank.

## Climate

Laos is a warm, tropical country with three seasons. A cool, dry period lasts from November to February. From the middle of February to May, the weather grows hot. A rainy season lasts from May through October.

Two monsoons—seasonal rain-bearing winds—sweep across Southeast Asia each year. They have a big impact on the Laotian climate. The northeast monsoon delivers little rain. But it is responsible for cool breezes from November to mid-February. The southwest monsoon, which comes in May or June, brings cloudy skies and heavy rains. As much as 160 inches (406 centimeters) of rain drenches the Bolovens Plateau in southern Laos. At least 50 inches (127 cm) fall at many of the country's other elevations.

The rain comes in different forms in different areas. A fine, dustlike moisture blows through the mountains. For weeks, brief but heavy downpours fall at about the same time every day in the lowlands. Violent storms known as typhoons roll westward from the Pacific Ocean and through the South China Sea. But they weaken as they move inland through Vietnam and Laos.

Temperatures vary from season to season and from place to place in Laos. High in the Annamese Cordillera, nighttime readings can drop below freezing. In the lowlands, spring temperatures exceed 90°F (32°C) almost every day. Vientiane averages 70°F (21°C) in winter, 89°F (32°C) in spring, and 82°F (28°C) during the rainy season.

## ⊙ Flora and Fauna

Laos is home to many types of plants and animals. A variety of trees grow in the monsoon forests of southern Laos, where the climate is not wet enough for tropical rain forests. Loggers in Laos's tropical rain forests harvest teak, mahogany, and other tropical hardwoods in increasing numbers. But these rain forests still thrive in the highlands of northern and eastern Laos. High rainfall and humidity support these complex ecosystems.

Despite the loss of forest to logging and agriculture, Laos still has more safe, remote areas for animals than any other nation in Southeast Asia. Once described as the land of a million elephants, Laos has tame as well as wild elephant herds. Many types of

### A MILLION ELEPHANTS

Laos has one of the largest populations of wild Asian elephants in Southeast Asia. Asian elephants differ from their African cousins in several characteristics. They don't grow as large, have smaller ears, and have lighter skin. Male Asian elephants can stand up to 10.5 feet (3.2 m) tall and can weigh as much as 8,000 pounds (3,600 kilograms).

Because so many Laotians live in rural areas, conflicts between humans and elephants are common. When people farm the land where elephants roam, the animals have to find new homes and food sources. Often the elephants have no choice but to invade farmers' crops. This can damage the livelihood of the farmers and their families.

A tame Asian elephant, wearing traditional gear, stars in this parade in Vientiane. The parade is a celebration of the 650th anniversary of the city.

wild oxen, large cats (including tigers and leopards), birds, monkeys, and reptiles live in heavily forested areas. Insects include stinging wasps, scorpions, and many kinds of beetles. At least one hundred kinds of butterflies flutter throughout the country, even during dry months.

More than one hundred varieties of snakes live in Laos, some of which are venomous. At least half a dozen of these snakes—including kraits, coral snakes, and pythons—are dangerous to people. The king cobra, which is known to reach a length of 18 feet (5.5 m), is the longest venomous

Although the Laotian rock rat is a fairly new animal to Western science (it was first noted in 1996), locals have always known it as the Kha-nyou. The animal resembles a rat with a thick tail. But it looks and behaves so differently from other rodents that scientists placed it in a new family, *Laonastidae*, which means "inhabitant of stone." The Laotian rock rat lives in karst limestone formations of the Cammon Plateau.

Poisonous snakes such as this **king cobra** are common in Laos, so Laotians and their guests watch where they walk. The Queen Saovabha Memorial Institute in Bangkok, Thailand, is the nearest manufacturer of king cobra antivenom (cure for this poisonous snake's bite).

snake on Earth. The nonvenomous python can grow even longer, up to 30 feet (9 m).

## Natural Resources and Environmental Concerns

The forests of Laos are the nation's most profitable natural resource. The country's most common mineral of value is tin, which is mined in the west central panhandle. Gypsum, a mineral used in making plaster, is another major resource. Stocks of salt are mined on a small scale. The coal deposits of northern Laos are largely untouched because there is no way to transport coal to processing centers. Laos also has undeveloped stocks of gold, zinc, lead, and silver, as well as petroleum reserves.

Dams on Laos's many rivers harness the rushing water to make hydroelectric power, a valuable energy resource. These rivers also yield more than 20,000 tons (18,143 metric tons) of fish each year. Fish species range from finger-sized types that are dried before being eaten to huge catfish that swim upriver in the Mekong.

These restaurants serve fresh fish. Ban Muang's ferry crossing on the Mekong River is an excellent fishing location.

While hydroelectric power is important to the economy of Laos, it also poses a danger to the environment. Dams change the way a river flows. They cause large backups of water that flood huge areas. The flooding destroys the homes of both people and wildlife.

Another environmental concern is deforestation (the loss of forest area due to agriculture and logging). Many of Laos's forests are still recovering from damage that occurred in its civil war and during the Vietnam War (1957–1975). Chemical sprays and bombs destroyed forests throughout Southeast Asia during the Vietnam War. In addition, farmers threaten the country's woodlands by cutting down trees and burning vegetation to clear land for growing crops. This technique, known as slash-and-burn farming, causes the biggest loss of Laos's forests. The government has taken steps to slow deforestation, including a program that set aside 42 million acres (17 million hectares) of land for preservation. The government has also banned the export of unprocessed timber and has passed laws to curb uncontrolled logging. But these measures have not stemmed the export of wood products, and the forests continue to shrink.

In a technique called **slash-and-burn farming,** Laotians cut down trees and burn vegetation on about 741,000 acres (300,000 hectares) annually. To limit this loss, Laos has set aside 11,200 square miles (29,000 sq. km) of forest, woodlands, streams, and rivers as National Biodiversity Conservation Areas.

French colonial buildings line **Fa Ngum Street in Vientiane.**

## Cities

Only about 20 percent of Laos's 6.2 million people live in urban areas. Laotian cities feature two-story stucco buildings that serve as both shops and houses. Two-story brick structures, dating to the French colonial period, also line some streets. Many houses are made of inexpensive and plentiful woods such as palm and bamboo. Others are made of palm thatch (woven palm fronds), especially in less-developed areas. More costly homes are made of teak and other tropical hardwoods.

VIENTIANE, the nation's capital, is the largest city. Compared to other capitals in Southeast Asia, Vientiane (estimated population 633,000) is small and quiet, having survived the wars of the mid-1900s mostly untouched. The city features tree-lined streets, well-preserved temples, and many structures dating from the French colonial period.

Located along the Mekong River in central Laos, Vientiane has existed for almost one thousand years. The city has seen Burmese, Khmer (Cambodian), Siamese (Thai), and Vietnamese rulers. Throughout Laotian history, Vientiane vied with Louangphrabang as the capital city. In 1893, under French control, Vientiane became the permanent capital. A few French-speaking residents still call the city home.

When the Communist Pathet Lao took control of Vientiane in 1975, they shut down most businesses—a move that prompted some residents to flee. After economic reforms began in the 1980s, Vientiane again benefited from its location along the busy Mekong. In the 1990s and early 2000s, small shops and other kinds of private businesses have added some bustle to the city's streets. The country's leading commercial center, Vientiane boasts many busy hotels, restaurants, and street markets, as well as a growing population. Some Laotians fear that increased development will overwhelm the city with new construction, overcrowding, and competition for jobs.

SAVANNAKHET (estimated population 105,000) also lies along the Mekong River. This city lies about 200 miles (322 km) downriver from Vientiane. Savannakhet's small business district sits near a river dock. From this dock, a ferry moves passengers and handmade Laotian ceramics across the Mekong to Thailand. The city features attractive European- and Asian-style buildings, as well as Buddhist wats (temples) and a Catholic church.

The Ho Chi Minh Trail, built during the Vietnam War, was a network of roads running from North Vietnam through Laos and Cambodia to South Vietnam. The trail provided support to the North Vietnamese army. Although decades of forest growth have hidden much of the trail, portions of the path are still visible.

Since the late nineteenth century, when the French took over Indochina as a colony, Savannakhet has included a large Vietnamese community. Many of these people worked in civil service positions for the French government. The rest of the city's population is a mix of Khmer, Chinese, various Laotian ethnic minorities, and a small number of Europeans. Foreign travelers use Savannakhet as a starting point for travel to the Ho Chi Minh Trail, a famous Vietnam War supply route that passed in and out of Laos.

SECONDARY CITIES The French founded Pakxe (estimated population 60,000) in 1905. This city lies north of the Cambodian border along the Mekong River. It is one of the few areas where both banks of the Mekong belong to Laos. Boats and trucks carry lumber from Pakxe to markets in Thailand. Many Pakxe residents are ethnically Chinese or Vietnamese.

Louangphrabang, a well-preserved and historic city of about 22,000 people, is north of Vientiane. Bicycles outnumber motor vehicles in Louangphrabang. Visitors there can visit dozens of historic wats and other religious sites. The city became the seat of the Lao monarchy in A.D.1353. It continued to be the home of members of the Lao royal family until 1975, when the Communists overthrew the last Laotian king.

 Visit www.vgsbooks.com for links to more information about urban and rural Laos.

# HISTORY AND GOVERNMENT

Although people have lived in Laos for thousands of years, its recorded history begins only in the fourteenth century A.D. Evidence of the people and rulers of earlier times exists in artifacts, in accounts written in other regions such as China, and in ancient legends passed on by the culture's storytellers.

## ○ First Settlers

Archaeologists believe that hunters and gatherers living north of the Plain of Jars were the first settlers on the Indochinese Peninsula. Taking advantage of the protection offered by caves, these people lived in the mountains rather than in the plains and river valleys. As their numbers grew, the people gradually moved to the Plain of Jars and other lowlands. There they kept herds of cattle and raised rice and other grain crops.

By 2000 B.C., the early people of Laos were building settlements in the Mekong River valley. Using bronze-making techniques, settlers created tools, weapons, and utensils. The people traded these useful items with other Southeast Asians and with the Chinese to the north. The making of iron began in the plains and valleys in about the fifth century B.C.

The early settlers eventually set up small chiefdoms, known as *mandalas*, in the Mekong River valley. Through trade in goods and food, these states came under the cultural influence of China as well as India, a large territory to the west. At the same time, the rugged mountains and remote forests of Laos saw little Indian or Chinese settlement. There, the descendants of the earliest peoples had little contact with the lowlands and were well beyond the reach of the new civilizations. For hundreds of years, the inhabitants of Laos lived peacefully, farming and trading in the country's valleys and highlands.

## Champa and Funan

By the late fifth century A.D., Indian settlers had founded Champa. Champa was a realm of small states. It stretched eastward from the central Mekong River valley, through portions of present-day Vietnam, to the

South China Sea. Its administrative hub—Champasak—lay on the western bank of the Mekong, near Laos's modern borders with Thailand and Cambodia. Indian newcomers brought Sanskrit, a written language, and Hinduism, a religion that stresses duty and individual destiny.

To the south of Champa was Funan, a rival state centered in modern Cambodia and the Mekong Delta of southern Vietnam. Although the founders of Funan were Khmer in origin, settlers from India also heavily influenced the state. The chief city of Funan, called Vyadhapura, was near the present-day Cambodian capital of Phnom Penh. Champa and Funan competed for power in Southeast Asia, but Funan had more success in the rivalry.

Late in the ninth century, in modern-day northwestern Cambodia, the Khmer established Angkor as the capital of a powerful empire known as Kambuja. The people who populated this realm controlled Cambodia as well as southern and central Laos. Elaborate stone Buddhist temples at Angkor symbolized the power of the Khmer culture.

The Khmer eventually enlarged Kambuja, while monks from present-day Thailand spread the new faith of Theravada Buddhism (teachings of the elders) to the central and upper Mekong. By the 1100s, the Khmer occupied the area of Vientiane, which centuries before had been a river-valley *muong* (district). As Khmer power expanded, the highland peoples of the north, called Kha (slaves), came under Kambuja's control. But soon a new wave of migration from the north checked the expansion of the Khmer states.

## ◉ Tai Migrations

The new immigration was the result of centuries of movement farther north. For centuries, ethnic Tai peoples of southern China and northern Vietnam had been traveling south from their empire of Nan Chao. Gradually, the Tai arrived in central Laos. They intermarried with the inhabitants of the area's forests and mountains. According to legend, a Tai prince founded the Louangphrabang principality (realm of a prince). He descended from Khoun Lo, the seventh son of a ruler of Nan Chao.

Since ancient times, each group of Tai hill dwellers in northern Laos has been identified by the color of clothing worn by its women. If the women of the village wear red, the group is known as Red Tai. A village is Black Tai if its women wear black.

Historians in China and Vietnam gave a new name—Lao—to the small principalities built by the migrating Tai (the ethnic Lao are a branch of the ethnic Tai people). From China the Tai brought new methods of agriculture to Laos. They cut away hillsides to create flat terraces on which to grow crops. They also built canals and irrigation systems to water rice paddies.

The Tai spread throughout Southeast Asia, setting up new principalities in Vietnam, Burma, Siam, and as far west as India. But by the 1200s, the Tai kingdom was under attack by Kublai Khan. He was a Mongol warlord from the plains of central Asia. In 1253 he destroyed Nan Chao. This event prompted a new wave of refugees to move into the land of the Mekong River valley.

A **Mongol warrior** could shoot a bow and arrow accurately from the back of a galloping horse. Mongol ruler Kublai Khan controlled an empire that stretched from eastern China to the Caspian Sea in western Asia. Kublai Khan's raids of the Tai kingdom in the 1200s forced refugees into the Mekong River valley.

## ◉ Fa Ngum

Rivalry between the Tai people of Louangphrabang and the Khmer people of Kambuja led to the first unified state in Laos. In the fourteenth century, Fa Ngum, a Tai prince who had grown up in the imperial courts of Angkor, married the daughter of Jayavarman Paramesvara, the king of Kambuja. Seeing an opportunity to expand his power, Jayavarman supplied Fa Ngum with an army. Fa Ngum then sent the army northward to conquer Louangphrabang, which fell in 1353.

The army's success allowed Fa Ngum to found the kingdom of Lan Xang, which means "Million Elephants." He expanded Lan Xang to include the lowlands east of the Mekong River and the plains of present-day northeastern Thailand. Fa Ngum made Theravada Buddhism the official religion of his realm.

Under Fa Ngum's orders, a mission to Angkor brought back a golden statue of the Buddha, the founder of Buddhism, called the Prabang. Said to have magical powers, the Prabang would become a sacred symbol of the Laotian state. It moved with the royal court whenever the court changed locations.

Fa Ngum's son, Sam Sen Thai, took over rule of Lan Xang in 1373. He oversaw the building of Buddhist wats throughout the kingdom. He expanded Lan Xang and recruited a powerful army of 150,000 foot soldiers, horsemen, and elephant drivers. At the same time, Siam overran Kambuja. As Lan Xang grew, it began to rival Siam and Burma, the two other major states in Southeast Asia.

## ◉ Regional Rivalries

Never as powerful as its larger neighbors, Lan Xang suffered frequent attacks by Siamese and Burmese armies. By the 1500s, the Lan Xang prince Setthathirath was fighting both the Burmese and the Khmer. To protect his territory, the king moved his capital from Louangphrabang to Vientiane. Vientiane was more central to Lao territories and easier to defend against Burmese attack. The Burmese successfully invaded Lan Xang anyway in 1563. They occupied the area for two years. During a battle in 1571, Setthathirath mysteriously disappeared.

Without a strong leader, Lan Xang was open to further attack. The Burmese soon conquered the kingdom. They made it a vassal state (one that pays tribute to a stronger power). A succession of Burmese rulers, as well as Laotian allies of Burma, took power in Lan Xang. Meanwhile, conflict over the succession to the throne of Lan Xang prompted invasions. The armies of Siam and of Vietnam—which had overrun Champa by this time to become a power in the region—staked their claims to the land. For twenty years, the region experienced nearly constant warfare.

A **monument dedicated to Prince Setthathirath** *(left)* **in Vientiane** features a statue of him on top. He built Pha That Luang *(right)* in 1566. Also known as the Great Stupa, this ornate structure is a Buddhist temple.

This chaotic period ended in 1591 when Kokeo Koumane became the king of Lan Xang. By 1603 this monarch was no longer paying tribute to Burma. Lan Xang was again an independent state. But internal power struggles continued for many years. The conflicts ended in 1637, when the Lao king Souligna Vongsa took power.

## The Golden Age

A strong ruler, Souligna Vongsa expanded and defined the borders of Lan Xang. He also lived in peace with the Burmese and the Vietnamese. A supporter of Buddhism and the arts, he built many monuments in Vientiane.

During Souligna Vongsa's reign, which Laotians consider the golden age of their history, European trading companies first arrived on the shores of Southeast Asia. The traders wanted to buy Asian goods to bring home to Europe. For example, Gerrit van Wuysthoff, an agent of a wealthy firm called the Dutch East India Company, visited the region in 1641. He brought the beginning of trade with the West. Soon afterward a Roman Catholic missionary from Italy, Giovanni Maria Leria, sought converts to his Christian faith in Souligna Vongsa's territory.

The death of Souligna Vongsa in 1694 brought about a crisis that would eventually lead to the downfall of Lan Xang. Vongsa's two grandsons—one of them a young man called Kitsarat—were next in line to rule. But because of their youth and inexperience, other highly placed officials fought over the throne.

At the same time, Sai Ong Hue, a nephew of Souligna Vongsa, asked the Vietnamese to help him win the crown. In exchange, Sai Ong Hue would allow the Vietnamese to make Lan Xang a vassal state. In 1700, at the head of a Vietnamese army, Sai Ong Hue captured Vientiane.

The **Dutch East India Company** had central offices in Hugli, West Bengal, India. The company operated from 1602 to 1795. In its time, it was the largest European trading company operating in Asia. The company also built forts, kept a standing army, appointed governors, and made treaties for the Dutch government.

## Division and Decline

The new king forced Kitsarat to flee Lan Xang. But Kitsarat soon returned. He seized Louangphrabang and proclaimed himself king of northern Laos. Meanwhile, another relative established his own kingdom alongside the Mekong in Champasak. The result was the division of modern-day Laos into three kingdoms named after their capitals—Louangphrabang in the north, Vientiane in the center, and Champasak in the south.

For the next century, the three states constantly fought one another. They also fought with the kingdoms of Siam, Burma, and Vietnam. Burma invaded in the mid-1700s. Within a few years, the Siamese—seeking to protect themselves against a Burmese invasion—overran Vientiane. To symbolize Siam's new dominance in the region, the Siamese captured the Prabang statue. They took it to Bangkok, the Siamese capital.

By 1782 both Vientiane and Louangphrabang were vassals of Siam. Siamese governors ruled over the Laotian states. They also had the right to appoint the Laotian kings. Chou Anou, whom the Siamese chose as the king of Vientiane in 1805, first served Siam as

a military commander. But after becoming king, he began to stand against Siamese authority. In 1827 Chou Anou led a fight against Bangkok. The mission failed. The Laotian army was destroyed. Siam took revenge by destroying Vientiane. For the rest of the century, the former kingdom of Vientiane would be a province of Siam.

## Colonial Laos

While the Laotian states were in turmoil, another foreign power came on the scene. Searching for a river route to China, French explorers and traders traveled up the wide Mekong River in the mid-1800s. France took over southern Vietnam and Cambodia in the 1860s, hoping that the Mekong would be a dependable way to reach China's inland riches. France's dreams were dashed just north of the modern Laotian-Cambodian border, where the river passes through several miles of rocky falls and steep curves. Traveling farther upriver was impossible for the large boats that transported trading goods.

The rest of Vietnam came under French rule in 1884. Three years later, the Laotian kingdoms experienced a similar fate. French diplomats signed an agreement with Siam to appoint a French official who would operate from the city of Vientiane. The Laotian monarch there held onto his throne but had little power.

By 1893 France had claimed much of Southeast Asia—including Vietnam, Cambodia, and the three Laotian kingdoms—as French Indochina. The Laotian area was valuable because it served as a mountainous borderland between French Indochina and Siam and Burma. These two Asian realms had links with Great Britain, France's European rival. In 1899 the French united the Laotian territories into a single entity known as Laos. They made Sisavang Vong the country's crown prince (heir to the throne). He assumed the throne several years later, upon returning to Laos from schooling abroad.

But Laos was only a minor part of French Indochina. Compared to Vietnam, which had more economic potential and drew many French colonists, few French people settled in Laos. The tiny, landlocked colony remained poor, underdeveloped, and geographically isolated. Those French people who did move to Laos were mainly government officials and teachers.

**Sisavang Vong (1885–1959)** succeeded his father as king of Louangphrabang in 1904, although France still ruled the region.

Although a small class of French-educated Laotians arose, French or Vietnamese officials governed the colony with no help from the local population. Because of the remoteness of the country, its sparse population, and a general acceptance of foreign involvement, the Laotians escaped the harsh rule that the French were practicing in Vietnam.

The colonial regime in Laos changed during World War II (1939–1945). Japanese soldiers overwhelmed the French forces and took control of much of Southeast Asia. Most of the fighting took place far from Laos, however, because the Japanese sailed around Indochina instead of marching through it.

After the defeat of Japan in 1945, the French returned to Indochina. But throughout the war, the people of Southeast Asia had developed a strong interest in governing themselves. Rather than be ruled by foreigners, Prince Phetsarath Rattanavongsa—the son of King Sisavang Vong—fled the country. He and others seeking Laotian independence started a movement in Thailand (formerly Siam) to free Laos from French rule.

In Vietnam, meanwhile, a force known as the Viet Minh carried on their fight against the French soldiers. The Viet Minh opposed French occupation as well as the monarchy. They favored a Communist government. The various movements for self-rule in Southeast Asia worried the French. Their control of the region was slipping away.

## Independence and the Roots of Civil War

In hopes of calming the people, the French wrote a constitution for Laos in 1947. They claimed the document would make Laos independent. But the government in exile, led by Prince Phetsarath, believed otherwise. The prince asked his brother Prince Souvanna Phouma and his half brother Prince Souphanouvong to lead the fight for full independence.

In 1949 the exiled government, known as Lao Issara (Free Laos), kicked out Souphanouvong for his support of the Communist Viet Minh. Souphanouvong then traveled to northern Vietnam. There he joined the Viet Minh and proclaimed Laos the Democratic Republic of Laos. This declaration helped to create a revolutionary military organization in Laos—similar to the Viet Minh—known as the Pathet Lao (Land of Laos). At the same time, Souvanna Phouma returned to Laos. There, he joined a new royal government that the French had helped to set up.

Overwhelmed by its ongoing war with Vietnam, France eventually agreed to give Laos complete independence in 1953. That same year, with the support of Viet Minh troops, Prince Souphanouvong opened a Pathet Lao headquarters in northeastern Laos. The help of the

**French troops ride domesticated elephants in the jungles of Laos** in the early 1950s. In that decade, France gave up control of Laos and other Indochinese colonies.

Communist government of North Vietnam would continue to be important throughout the course of Laos's Communist struggle. In 1954 Vietnam defeated the French. At a postwar conference held in Geneva, Switzerland, France formally recognized the independence of all its former Indochinese colonies. The settlement gave the Pathet Lao control over two northern provinces. French-backed Laotian soldiers occupied the rest of Laos.

The year after France withdrew from French Indochina, the Kingdom of Laos joined the United Nations. The international community officially recognized Laos as an independent state. In spite of its newfound independence, however, Laos was far from unified. Power struggles and civil war would divide the country for the next twenty years. For example, when legislative elections took place in 1955, the Pathet Lao refused to participate. They reasoned that the royalists did not have authority to call for elections in the northern provinces. When Prince Souvanna Phouma became the prime minister of the new Laotian government in 1956, Prince Souphanouvong stayed in northern Laos with the Communist forces.

## Anti-Communist Activities

In time, Laos set up a coalition (cooperative) leadership, bringing Souphanouvong into the government. Elections in 1958 for the twenty-one assembly seats of the northern provinces resulted in thirteen wins by the Pathet Lao's political party, the Lao Patriotic Front. The United States, which was strongly anti-Communist, was unhappy with the election results. It threatened to cut off all aid to Laos. To satisfy U.S. concerns, conservative Laotians in the coalition government arrested Souphanouvong and other Communist leaders, though they later escaped.

To further oppose Communist influence, a group of Laotian leaders formed the U.S.-backed, anti-Communist Committee for the Defense of National Interests. In response, the Communist governments in the Soviet Union (a union of Russia and fourteen other republics) and in North Vietnam gave the Pathet Lao aid. As political conflict worsened, the entire Laotian government collapsed in 1958. A new anti-Communist regime took its place. Phoui Sananikone headed the new government, which refused to deal with the Pathet Lao. As with many of Laos's leaders during this turbulent era, his time in power was brief.

The continuing disagreement between the Laotian Communists and their opponents caused civil war to break out between royalists and Communists. The less-powerful neutralists favored neither side but wanted to bring about long-term political stability.

The ongoing conflict resulted in a complicated series of short-term governments. In 1960 a neutralist

## THE PATHET LAO

Prince Souphanouvong founded the Pathet Lao during the early 1950s as a political movement based on Communism. In its early years, the organization concentrated its efforts against capitalism and other Western governmental schools of thought. In 1975 the organization successfully achieved power in Laos and became the Lao People's Revolutionary Party. Later, the term *Pathet Lao* became a generic name for Laotian Communists.

military group led by Kong Le, a young soldier who had grown tired of the fighting, took control of Vientiane. The group set up a new government. Six months later, General Phoumi Nosavan overthrew Kong and made his anti-Communist ally Boun Oum the prime minister. Foreign powers including the United States and Thailand wanted to limit Communist influence in Southeast Asia. These powers armed the anti-Communists. Meanwhile, the Soviet Union and North Vietnam continued to supply the Pathet Lao.

## Gains by Communists

Nosavan's victory prompted the Pathet Lao to attack from their bases in northern Laos. In May 1961, the United States joined the Soviet Union and others in negotiating a cease-fire. In Geneva all sides agreed to a neutralist Government of National Unity under Souvanna Phouma.

The cease-fire lasted until April 1963, when the murder of a government minister renewed the fighting. During the next phase of the civil war, which lasted more than a decade, Souvanna Phouma struggled to run the country with members of the old neutralist administration.

From 1964 to 1973, conflicts erupted throughout Southeast Asia. The fighting was especially bad in Vietnam, where the United States was heavily involved. Because the United States had air bases in Thailand, U.S. planes frequently passed over Laos during bombing missions to Vietnam. Secret bombing of Pathet Lao regions was also common. In addition, the United States trained and supplied an army of nearly ten thousand soldiers for battle against the Pathet Lao forces. Most of these soldiers were Hmong, an ethnic group that included mainly royalists.

Throughout the Vietnam War, Laotian officials firmly believed that the outcome of the war would decide their own future. If the Communists were successful in Vietnam and Cambodia, three of Laos's neighbors—China, Vietnam, and Cambodia—would be Communist nations. Laotian politicians prepared as best they could for an uncertain future.

Souvanna Phouma's government opened negotiations with the Pathet Lao in 1972. In early 1973, as the United States was pulling out of Vietnam and the region, the two sides agreed to a cease-fire. Several coalition governments tried without success to run the country, and fighting continued in Laos between royalist soldiers and the Pathet Lao.

When the Communist movements in Vietnam and Cambodia were victorious in 1975, anti-Communist Laotians fled to

A **U.S. Air Force F-5 fighter drops its bombs over a target in Vietnam** in 1966. During the Vietnam War, bombers from U.S. military bases in Thailand flew across Laos to reach Vietnam.

Thailand. The Pathet Lao finally took control of Vientiane in August 1975. The takeover was a surprisingly bloodless finish to what had been a long and bloody civil war.

## The Lao People's Democratic Republic

In December 1975, the new leaders declared the founding of the Lao People's Democratic Republic (LPDR). The new government allied with the Soviet Union and China, two powerful Communist nations that had supported the Communist efforts in Southeast Asia. To enforce the change in power, the Pathet Lao cut most communications with the outside world. They sent former government officials and members of the royalist army to work camps. At the camps, the Pathet Lao forced inmates to learn Communist ideas.

Prince Souphanouvong, a supporter of the Pathet Lao, became the new president. He and other LPDR leaders, who had long been aligned with the Communist government of Vietnam, allowed thousands of Vietnamese troops to come inside Laos. Because Vietnam and China

> Learn more about the history of Laos. Go to www.vgsbooks.com for links.

were not on good terms, the presence of Vietnamese forces made relations with China difficult. China quickly withdrew aid to Laos. However, Laos continued to receive help from the Soviet Union and its allies in Eastern Europe.

The postwar economic situation in Laos was bleak. Laos lost all aid from the United States, which had supported the anti-Communists. The LPDR took over private businesses and combined small farms into huge agricultural collectives (groupings). Economic help from fellow Communist countries increased, but the Laotian economy remained weak. It was dependent on foreign aid and dominated by farming.

Alliances with Communist countries continued to benefit Laos throughout the 1980s. But the nation's economy was unable to recover from the years of civil unrest. Younger Communists felt the need for change. Governmental reforms slowly replaced outdated Communist policies, and Laos held a national election in 1988.

LPDR leaders began to release political prisoners, including many Hmong citizens who had fought against the Pathet Lao during the war. But the continuing activities of a conservative political group called the United Lao National Liberation Front slowed these improvements. Headed by Outhong Sougannavong, the group claimed to have liberated (freed from Communist rule) large pieces of Laotian territory in the 1980s under the direction of the Hmong general Vang Pao. Government soldiers and Vang's troops clashed.

Despite this conflict, the Lao People's Revolutionary Party, the only legal political party in Laos, went ahead with its plans to hold a

## MOVING TOWARD FREEDOM

**For fifteen years after the 1975 revolution, Laos operated without a constitution. But in August 1991, the nation approved a new constitution. The document highlights freedom and basic democratic rights. It also changed the country's motto from "Peace, Independence, Unity, and Socialism," to "Peace, Independence, Democracy, Unity, and Prosperity." These changes showed the rest of the world that Laos intended to pursue some freedom and democratic rights for the Lao people.**

congress (general meeting) in 1991. The party's core group, the central committee, runs the party, which in turn runs the country. During the congress, earlier economic reforms were broadened. The changes pushed the country away from a centralized system. The reforms inched Laos toward a free-market economy, in which buyers and sellers—not the government—determine what is sold and at what price. The committee decided that economic reform should be one of the country's main goals. They created a new constitution that allowed private ownership of property. This document was the country's first constitution since the LPDR had taken power in 1975. The new constitution allowed outside investors to own what they built or developed in Laos. Equally important were political reforms that reduced Vietnam's influence and its military personnel within Laos.

## Into the Twenty-First Century

In 1997 another big step for Laos was its admission into the Association of Southeast Asian Nations (ASEAN). This organization promotes regional cooperation, peace, and economic growth. Laos's leaders have continued their push for a more international economy that adds elements of capitalism into the Communist economy. In 1998 Khamtai Siphandon, the former leader of Pathet Lao, became the president of Laos. In 2001 he named Boungnang Volachit as the nation's prime minister. In 2004 Siphandon and Volachit helped Laos achieve another big economic goal, Normal Trade Relations status with the United States. This status gives Laos the ability to export goods to the United States and its rich markets.

Despite the nation's progress, the Laotian government still faces serious problems. Political and social reforms have come more slowly than economic changes. Although Laos's constitution guarantees human rights, reports indicate that basic freedoms—such as speech, assembly, travel, privacy and, to a degree, religion—are denied. In addition, political corruption and theft have drained the state of money and property.

In the early 2000s, Laos has concentrated on relations with its Indochinese neighbors. One example of regional cooperation is Laos and Thailand's efforts to build the Nam Theun II Dam on the Nam Theun River, scheduled for completion in 2009. While Laos welcomes such interaction, the small nation also worries about cultural domination from stronger, more developed lands such as Thailand. Foreigners, on the other hand, are eager to invest money in Laos. If government leaders can make progress in addressing

Laos's internal needs, foreign investment may bring a brighter economic future.

The summer of 2006 was a time of change for the Laotian government. Siphandon stepped down from the presidency. He was replaced by Choummaly Sayasone. Sayasone had previously served as Laos's vice president. Volachit, meanwhile, took over as vice president. He was replaced with a new prime minister, Bouasone Bouphavanh.

## Government

According to the 1991 constitution, the president is the highest-ranking government official in Laos. The National Assembly, the country's legislature, appoints the president to a five-year term. The president names a prime minister and the members of the Council of Ministers. This council directs the operations of the government's various ministries.

Legislative power belongs to the 109 elected members of the National Assembly. All citizens over the age of eighteen are eligible to vote. They elect these officials for a period of five years. The Lao People's Revolutionary Party continues to be the only legal

Residents of Hanoi, Vietnam, welcomed **Choummaly Sayasone** *(left front)* to their country on June 19, 2006. On his first trip abroad as president of Laos, Sayasone also traveled to Beijing to meet with Chinese leaders.

To keep up on current affairs in Laos, go to www.vgsbooks.com for links.

political party. Those who wish to run for office must be party members. On the local level, the president chooses governors to run the nation's sixteen provinces and one municipality.

Laos's judicial system includes the Supreme People's Court—the nation's highest court. The National Assembly chooses the members of this court. The legislature also appoints the judges of provincial and municipal courts. District and military courts operate with limited authority.

Laos divides itself into sixteen provinces. Each province is divided into districts, which are further divided into two or more subdistricts, or cantons. These subdistricts are often made up of several villages.

# THE PEOPLE

Laos is a largely rural nation. Less than 25 percent of its 6.2 million people live in large cities. Laos has about 68 persons per square mile (26 per sq. km). The country is one of the most sparsely populated nations in all of Asia. Many Laotians are lowlanders who make a living as farmers. The rivers that provide irrigation for rice growing run through narrow east-west valleys, keeping the people isolated from one another. As a result, languages and customs may differ from one valley to the next. Isolated living conditions are common for mountain-dwelling people as well.

The population of Laos is young. About 42 percent of the people are fourteen years of age or younger. The number of Laotians is also growing rapidly. The high birthrate is partly due to the government's ban on birth control. At the annual growth rate of 2.4 percent, the country's population will double in less than thirty years. If that rate of growth continues in the long term, the larger population could put a great strain on the nation's food supply.

## Ethnic Groups

Laos has as many as sixty-eight ethnic groups living within its borders. About 68 percent of this population is ethnic Lao Lum, often referred to simply as Lao. The Lao Theung (also called Mon-Khmer) makes up about 22 percent of the population. The Lao Soung (including the Hmong and the Mien peoples) makes up about 9 percent. Ethnic Vietnamese, Chinese, and other groups make up the remaining 1 percent.

The Lao, often called lowlanders, live mainly at lower elevations. Most Lao live in rural areas or in small villages. Their households are often large and hold three or more generations. As the household grows, the family adds new rooms. The people build their houses on stilts—a precaution against flooding caused by monsoon rains.

The Lao Theung is a grouping that includes at least thirty-seven different ethnic subgroups. The largest of these subgroups, the

## THE OLD WAYS

Many rural villages of Laos have remained untouched for centuries. In these communities, two seasons dictate the rhythm of life: rainy and dry. May brings the southwest monsoon rains, beginning the planting season. During the growing season, the men fish and hunt while the women grow vegetables and weave. The work continues until October, when it is time to harvest. In most areas, farmers still use oxen and hand tools for field work rather than modern tractors and other machinery.

Kammu, has about 400,000 members. Smaller subgroups such as the Numbri may have 100 members or fewer. Most Lao Theung families are rice farmers. They often live in small villages but are also known as a nomadic people who frequently move from place to place.

The Lao Soung is made up of six ethnic groups, the largest of which is the Hmong. The name *Lao Soung* means "the Lao (people) up high," and the group is often called highlanders or hill people. They tend to live at high elevations, including mountaintops, upland ridges, or hillsides. These people are also the newest to Laos. They came from China and Vietnam within the past two hundred years.

## Language and Education

Laos has three major languages associated with ethnic groups. Most lowlanders speak Lao, the nation's official tongue, which is close to the language spoken in Thailand. Written Lao uses a modified form of the Sanskrit alphabet. The language itself is tonal. This means that a one-syllable word can have different meanings, depending on the speaker's pitch of voice. Meanwhile, the Lao Theung speak Lao Theung, a language similar to Mon-Khmer, the language of Cambodia. Likewise, the Lao Soung speak their own language—Lao Soung.

Careful listeners also may hear other languages throughout Laos. In Vientiane a small number of older Laotians use French. In contrast, Tibeto-Burman languages are common along the border with Myanmar and China. Thai, Chinese, and Vietnamese people living in Laos may use the languages of their home countries. Some people also speak English, mainly in business and government centers in Vientiane and along the Mekong River.

All children between the ages of seven and fifteen are supposed to attend school. But many parents ignore this law—especially among the hill people, who are often on the move and may not settle down long enough to enroll children in school. Many of these children work

The message on this hand-painted sign is written in both Lao and English.

in the fields with their parents instead of attending school. The official language, Lao, is spoken in most schools. Literacy in Laos is on the rise, in part because of the addition of private schools in the nation. About 66 percent of the people can read and write. Literacy figures are higher for males (about 77 percent) than for females (about 55 percent). Laotian families traditionally have felt it more important to educate sons than daughters.

Few Laotian students are schooled beyond the age of fifteen. Laos has only one university, the National University of Laos in Vientiane. Founded in 1996, the university includes nine different colleges, each devoted to a different subject. Students can earn degrees in teaching, forestry, agriculture, communications, and more.

Find out more about the many ethnic groups living in Laos and learn about its language, education, and health. Visit www.vgsbooks.com for links.

## Health

Tropical diseases, isolation, malnutrition, and poverty challenge the Laotian medical system. The infant mortality rate (the number of babies who die within their first year) is 85 in every 1,000 live births. This number is high for Southeast Asia. The life expectancy rate for Laotians is 53 years for men and 56 years for women, lower than the figures for most Southeast Asian countries.

Although improved medical care has helped to reduce the infant mortality rate, illnesses such as malaria and hemorrhagic fever are still problems. Other diseases—deadly if left untreated—include dysentery, hepatitis, and tuberculosis. No national immunization program exists. The area is also at risk for new strains of flu, such as the bird flu that gained international attention in the early 2000s. Laos's isolation is partly responsible, however, for the nation's low incidence of acquired immunodeficiency syndrome (AIDS), caused by the human immunodeficiency virus (HIV). Only about 0.1 percent of Laotians have the disease.

The rice-based Laotian diet lacks proteins and minerals, and resulting malnutrition puts people at risk for catching diseases. In addition, clean drinking water isn't available in many areas and sanitation can

This **irrigation canal near Vientiane** may have fertilizer and other pollutants in it. Yet Laotians wash their clothes in this water. They may further risk their health by drinking canal water and bathing in it. Clean drinking water is hard to find in many places.

be poor. Another health hazard, particularly among hill people and loggers, is injury and death from unexploded bombs and shells left from the civil war era.

Drug addiction is an additional health problem for the people of Laos. For years the nation had one of the highest abuse rates of opium and heroin in the world. But the number of addicts dropped sharply in the early 2000s. In 1999, as many as sixty thousand Laotians had an opium addiction. By 2006, that figure had dropped to about twelve thousand.

With the help of the United Nations, Laos has opened centers to help people overcome these dangerous addictions. Drug officials from Myanmar and Thailand have also agreed to work with Laos to stop drug use and production. To encourage farmers to stop growing poppies (used to produce opium and heroin) and to cultivate other crops, the government has set up rural development programs. The programs have made a big impact, sharply reducing opium production in the early 2000s. In 1998 an estimated 66,200 acres (26,800 hectares) of land in Laos was used to grow poppies for opium. By 2006 that number had been reduced to 6,200 acres (2,500 hectares).

Because of a poor road system, transportation to hospitals and clinics is difficult. Doctors are also in short supply. A study found that there were only 558 doctors, 2,346 medical workers, and 6,600 first-aid workers in the country. Most of the nation's health-care workers are in or near Vientiane. Good care is difficult to find in remote areas.

## A BLOODY LEGACY

In the decades following the end of the conflicts Indochina (including the Laotian civil war), more than eleven thousand people have been killed, and many more injured, by unexploded bombs and shells. Many of these deaths occur when villagers in rural areas disturb the bombs while doing everyday activities such as digging up fields or looking for firewood. Commonly, these poor villagers are killed while attempting to salvage the metal from the bombs to sell.

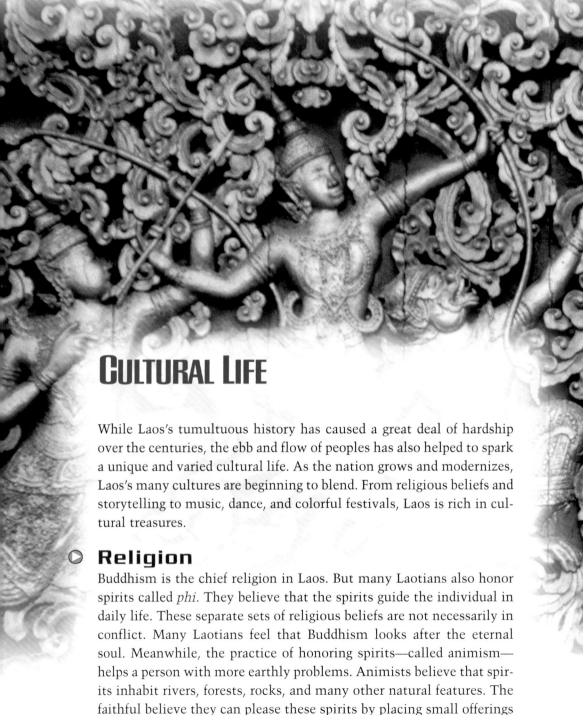

# CULTURAL LIFE

While Laos's tumultuous history has caused a great deal of hardship over the centuries, the ebb and flow of peoples has also helped to spark a unique and varied cultural life. As the nation grows and modernizes, Laos's many cultures are beginning to blend. From religious beliefs and storytelling to music, dance, and colorful festivals, Laos is rich in cultural treasures.

## Religion

Buddhism is the chief religion in Laos. But many Laotians also honor spirits called *phi*. They believe that the spirits guide the individual in daily life. These separate sets of religious beliefs are not necessarily in conflict. Many Laotians feel that Buddhism looks after the eternal soul. Meanwhile, the practice of honoring spirits—called animism—helps a person with more earthly problems. Animists believe that spirits inhabit rivers, forests, rocks, and many other natural features. The faithful believe they can please these spirits by placing small offerings

of food, little flags, and incense in obvious places. While many people consider themselves both Buddhists and animists, statistics list the population as 60 percent Buddhist and 40 percent other religions. This grouping is primarily animist but also includes Christians, Hindus, and others. Some people follow no religion.

Buddhism began in India in the sixth century B.C. The faith traces its origins to Siddhartha Gautama, a prince who went on a long search for the meaning of life. In time, Gautama became known as the Buddha, which means the "enlightened one." He won followers to his teachings in India. Buddhism became India's main religion. Early traders spread it to Thailand and across Southeast Asia. In the fourteenth century A.D., King Fa Ngum declared Buddhism as the official religion of Laos. Buddhist wats and monks became important features of Laotian life. The type of Buddhism most common in Laos is Theravada Buddhism, which celebrates the ancient Buddhist traditions.

Laos is one of the few Communist nations in which Buddhists are allowed to openly practice their faith. Most Communist countries discourage religion. This openness to Buddhism may be because the religion's followers are taught to reject material wealth, a philosophy in line with Communist ideas. Regardless of the cause, Laotian Buddhists fared much better than their counterparts in Cambodia, where a repressive government burned temples and killed Buddhist monks.

Ethnic Chinese and Vietnamese people practice a blend of Buddhism and Chinese Confucianism, a social philosophy that values proper behavior and social order. Christian missionaries converted some hill people to Christianity in the 1950s, and a small portion of the Laotian population remains Christian. Since the Communist revolution of 1975, the government has not allowed

**Many rural people in Laos still observe the Lao Buddhist calendar, which follows the movements of the sun and the moon. Under this calendar, the new year begins in April.**

Lao soldiers line up for a parade in Vientiane. The event, on December 2, 2005, celebrated the thirtieth anniversary of Communism in Laos.

religious missionary work. Foreigners trying to convert Laotians have been fined and ordered out of the country.

## Festivals, Literature, and the Arts

Buddhism has no regular religious services. But Laotians observe various holidays with festivals at the village pagoda, or temple. To celebrate the Buddha's birth, the Buddha's death, the Laotian New Year, and other important dates, people gather to enjoy music, food, and drink. They often set off rockets and fireworks. These festive occasions provide opportunities for young, unmarried men and women from nearby villages to meet.

Plays and puppet shows often use stories from the nation's most popular piece of literature, the *Ramayana*, as their inspiration. Originating in India, this Hindu epic poem tells of dashing heroes, vengeful gods, nasty demons, monkey armies, and more.

For centuries, oral folktales made up most of Laos's literature. Buddhist monks used storytelling to spread their faith. These stories comprised the *Jataka*, a set of tales about previous incarnations (lives) of the Buddha. The most famous of these tales was *Vessantara*, named for the central character, Prince Vessantara, a future incarnation of the Buddha.

Because printing technology didn't arrive in Laos until the 1920s, its history of written literature is short. Pierre Somchine Nginn wrote Laos's first modern novel, *Phra Phoutthahoup Saksit* (*The Sacred Buddha Image*) in 1944. In the late 1990s and early 2000s, Outhine Bounyavong was Laos's most popular writer. His short story collections, including 1999's *Mother's Beloved*, have been printed worldwide.

One of the most important pieces of Laotian literature is the *Vessantara*. It tells of Vessantara, a generous prince who is an incarnation of the future Buddha. Prince Vessantara's generous spirit becomes a burden. He keeps giving until he has given everything he owns—even his children. But in the end, his children are returned and he is blessed with plenty of wealth to give away.

The Buddhist religion heavily influences much of Laos's art, literature, and other culture. Although well known for ornamentation, Laos does not have a wide range of art. For centuries the Communist government closely controlled artistic expression. In addition, decades of bombing destroyed much of the country's ancient carvings, sculptures, and other pieces of art.

## ◎ Crafts

Laos has a strong tradition of handmade crafts. The hill people of Laos produce striking jewelry and cloth. They hammer silver or pewter into necklaces, earrings, bracelets, and other objects. Many highlanders wear handwoven scarves. Handmade rugs depict religious and spiritual scenes. Many Hmong embroider intricate tapestries called story cloths. Through images, these cloths tell stories about a family or village.

Pottery also has been a popular art form for centuries. Intricately designed tiles, jars, plates, and teapots in a wide variety of sizes are common throughout Laos. Perhaps the most famous works of pottery are the ancient, huge containers that dot the Plain of Jars.

### DRESSED FOR SUCCESS

In most Laotian societies, the women are responsible for making clothing for the whole family. They use looms about 10 feet (3 m) long and 6 feet (2 m) tall, and they often work outside for the best light. Weavers design complicated patterns, which often represent cultural symbols and incorporate historical stories. Mothers, grandmothers, and aunts pass on this art form to girls as young as four. Women from different ethnic groups have begun to exchange patterns and designs. Some have started selling their clothing at local markets.

Women from northern Laos sell their textiles and embroidery at the local market in Louangphrabang.

**Northern Laos's ethnic minorities produce brightly colored textiles** in a
variety of traditional designs.

Wood carving is another long-standing Laotian tradition. Because the nation is heavily forested, locals have plenty of raw materials with which to work. Religious carvings, including Buddha figures, are a popular theme. Examples of the nation's finest wood carving can be found at many Buddhist temples. The intricate carvings adorn temple doors, pillars, and more. Other examples of the craft, such as tables, chairs, and cabinets, are more practical.

 View more examples of Laotian crafts and learn more about the nation's cultural life. Visit www.vgsbooks.com for links.

## Music and Dance

*Lam*, a kind of Lao folk music, is impromptu (unplanned and unrehearsed) singing with the *khene*, a bamboo pipe mouth organ. The khene is a big part of native Laotian music. It can be played solo or with other instruments. Sometimes large groups of khene players gather to form khene orchestras.

Orchestras have been a part of Laotian festivals for several centuries. Musical instruments include two-stringed violins with single-string bows, xylophones, drums, and lutes. More recently,

Women perform **a traditional dance at a Buddhist** *baci,* or well-wishing ceremony, in Louangphrabang.

Laotian musicians have also taken up accordions, banjos, and guitars. Recorded music heard on the radio or played from cassettes and CDs is threatening the existence of live orchestras, which remain popular for weddings and festivals.

The graceful *lamvong* dance often accompanies the music. Known outside Asia as Thai-style dancing, lamvong is a folk dance in which participants move slowly in a large circle, often on or around a platform built especially for the occasion. The dancers' hands slowly shoot imaginary arrows, play imaginary instruments, and beckon audiences.

## Sports and Recreation

The people of Laos work hard to survive. Many of them don't have the time for recreation and leisure that people in wealthier nations have. But Laotians still set aside some time to enjoy themselves. Sports, music, and festivals are among the nation's many pastimes.

Many of the games of Laos are unique to Southeast Asia. One popular game is called *takraw*. Played with a hollow cane ball, takraw is like a cross between volleyball and soccer. The object is for players to keep the ball moving over a net using only their feet, shoulders, and elbows. Lao-style boxing is a martial art that pits two opponents against each other. It's a little like kickboxing, with the opponents using their hands and feet to try to score a knock-down.

As in most nations around the world, soccer (also called football) is popular in Laos. The Laos national team, which wears red, white, and blue, is a member of the Asian Football Confederation. The team made it to the second round of qualifying for the 2006 World Cup, a worldwide soccer competition. It was an exciting accomplishment for soccer fans in Laos.

**Laotian soccer** player Kaysone Soukhavong *(right)* fights an Indonesian player for the ball at the 2005 Southeast Asian (SEA) Games in Bacolod, Philippines.

The produce section of the **Phousi open-air market in Louangphrabang** offers shoppers a wide variety of foods.

Other pastimes in Laos include shopping at markets, visiting with friends and family, attending festivals, making crafts, and going to movies. While Laos doesn't have its own film industry, many cities have theaters and bring in movies from China or India.

## ⊙ Food

Because most people in Laos farm rice, their lives often center on the growth and harvest of that food. Farmers grow rice both in the lowlands (wet rice) and the highlands (dry rice). Families serve it with almost every meal. The rice is sticky enough to be rolled into a small ball and eaten with the hands.

Few Laotian households have refrigeration, so most people shop daily for fresh food at street markets. Laotians commonly eat water buffalo, pork, or chicken just hours after butchers slaughter the animals. Also popular are prepared foods such as *foe* (rice noodle soup). Offered from a pushcart, this dish includes steaming broth, noodles, bits of beef, herbs, and slices of onion. Fruits popular among Laotians include bananas, guavas, papayas, pineapples, and plums. Citrus fruits, such as grapefruits, lemons, and oranges, are common.

Laotians also dine on freshwater fish. Flavorings include strong-smelling fish sauce (a condiment made from fermented fish), limes, and chilies that range from mild to very hot. They often serve the fish with a variety of vegetables and noodles. French-style bread is available in Vientiane and other large cities. In these cities, a European breakfast of a roll, jam, and coffee is gaining in popularity. A popular dessert in Laos is *nam van mak kuay*. This treat, served cold, includes bananas, coconut milk, tapioca, and sugar.

The Lao national dish is *larb*, a type of meat salad. Made with almost any type of meat, larb takes much of its flavor from fish sauce, chili, mint, and lime. The meat in the dish can be either raw or cooked. Like most meals in Laos, larb is served with vegetables and sticky rice.

Laos has one brewery, which distributes beer to major cities within the country. There are also several soft drinks on the market. One of the most popular beverages is sugarcane juice, which vendors often prepare fresh on street corners. Other common drinks are soy milk, coconut milk, and fruit juice. People also enjoy locally grown coffee and tea.

## LARB

The national dish of Laos is easy to make and works with many meats. This recipe uses pork. Be careful handling hot chilies. Their juice can burn your eyes. Shop for lemongrass and Asian chili sauce at an Asian market. Laotians serve larb with rice and vegetables.

1 tablespoon peanut oil

1 pound ground pork

2 green chilies (such as jalapeños), finely diced and seeds removed

2 stems of lemongrass (white parts only), chopped

4 cloves of garlic, chopped

¼ cup lime juice

2 teaspoons lime rind (grated lime peel)

1 teaspoon Asian chili sauce

⅓ cup cilantro (coriander leaves), chopped

¼ cup chopped mint

1 small red onion, finely sliced

⅓ cup roasted, unsalted peanuts

Several lettuce leaves

1. Heat the oil in a wok (round bottom pan) or large skillet.
2. Stir the pork, chilies, lemongrass, and garlic over high heat until the pork is cooked (at least 6 minutes).
3. Place the mixture into a bowl, and stir in the lime juice, lime rind, chili sauce, cilantro, mint, onion, and peanuts.
4. Arrange lettuce leaves on plates, and spoon the mixture on top of them.

Serves 4

# THE ECONOMY

After Laos's civil war ended in 1975, the country faced serious economic problems. One of the poorest nations in Southeast Asia, Laos had a low standard of living. Most farm families produced only enough food to eat. This form of agriculture, called subsistence farming, leaves no extra crops to sell at markets.

With most people involved in agriculture, little opportunity existed to develop other sectors of the economy. In addition, the government's Communist policies—including state ownership of businesses—slowed foreign investment. The nation desperately needed the outside income to build and modernize its industries. Furthermore, because it was aligned with Vietnam, Laos suffered poor relations with its more powerful neighbors—Thailand and China.

During its early years among the world's Communist nations, Laos got economic aid chiefly from the Soviet Union and Vietnam. Laotian leaders realized, however, that they could not depend on

outsiders for their country's long-term well-being. By 1980 reformers had introduced new policies that relaxed the government's tight economic controls.

The government's New Economic Mechanism loosened its ban on private ownership in 1986. Soon afterward, privately owned small stores began to open, first in Vientiane and then in other cities. In 1988 foreign investment in Laos became legal. By the mid-1990s, foreign businesses were springing up throughout Laos, where labor is cheap and plentiful. That trend continues into the 2000s.

Free-trade reforms have also led to rapid development. To enhance this growth, the Laotian government has joined the Association of Southeast Asian Nations. Membership in this trading group helps promote foreign investment in Laos. It also helps to pull Laos's leaders and its people into a more modern, worldwide economy.

## Agriculture and Forestry

Agriculture, including forestry, makes up 50 percent of the Laotian gross domestic product (GDP)—the total value of all goods and services produced in a year. Timber and sawn wood account for almost 40 percent of all exports. Laos also sells fruits, vegetables, and grains abroad. But food production remains an ongoing problem, with imports of food still outpacing exports.

Even though 80 percent of Laos's population relies on agriculture to make a living, less than 10 percent of the country's total land area is usable.

To feed its people, Laos depends heavily on its annual harvest of rice. Rice fields occupy 85 percent of all the nation's cultivated land. But when droughts, floods, and pests cause poor harvests, reports of malnutrition are common. The country must sometimes accept foreign aid, even to supply provinces that usually have good harvests.

Laotian farmers also grow corn, cassavas, potatoes, cotton, tobacco, and coffee. Pigs are the most common farm animal. Other

**Pigs roam freely in this village near Pakxe.** They are the most common farm animals in Laos.

livestock includes buffalo, poultry, and cattle. Aquaculture (fish farming) is another important industry. About half of all farming is done on state-run farms. On these farms, growers share the work and the income from harvests. Private farms account for the other half of agricultural production.

A big challenge facing Laos is the poor management of its forest resources. Continued deforestation is costing the nation much of its natural forests. The government has banned the export of unprocessed timber. It has also passed laws to reduce logging. Despite these measures, wood products remain one of the country's biggest exports.

The government is also dealing with the harvest of opium poppies. In remote valleys near the borders with Myanmar and China, Laotian villagers grow poppies. They cut the buds and collect the sap to sell to heroin processors. Laws in Laos ban the growing of poppies, but the government does little to enforce the regulations. As a result, northern Laos—a part of the so-called Golden Triangle—continues to be a source of the world's heroin.

## Manufacturing and Mining

Manufacturing and mining together contribute about 27 percent of Laos's GDP. Important manufactured goods include tires, textiles, clothing, plastic products, animal feed, bricks, beer, soft drinks, and soap powder. Most of the foods and drinks produced in Laos are sold within the country, while the nation exports most of the tires it produces.

When the Pathet Lao came into power in 1975, it set up a Communist economy. The government set prices, took control of private assets, and discouraged foreign trade. But in 1986, the government replaced this system with the New Economic Mechanism, a system closer to Western-style capitalism. The new system lifted trade barriers, ended price setting, and allowed farmers to own their land.

Thailand is by far the largest customer for Laotian goods. France, Germany, and Japan are among its other markets. Laos's main exports are timber and wood products, electricity, textiles and garments, coffee, tin, and gypsum. Despite a rise in exports, however, Laos still runs a trade deficit. This means that the country spends more on foreign goods than it receives for its exports. Thailand—the largest source of Laos's imports—supplies rice and consumer goods, ranging from electronics to vehicles, machinery, and construction equipment. Japan, China, and Italy also sell goods to Laos. Once closed to most foreign investment, Laos has passed laws making it easier for foreigners to invest or build in the country. Leading investors in Laos include Thailand, the United States, Australia, China, France, and Taiwan. Laos has sold land for the construction of hotels, casinos, and golf courses. Each year the government receives thousands of applications from foreign groups seeking to build everything from wood-production facilities to garment factories.

Tin and gypsum are the two most commonly mined minerals in Laos. Each year, the nation extracts more than 100 tons (91 metric tons) of both tin and gypsum. The nation also has several small salt mines, but production is minimal.

## Services and Tourism

Services make up about 23 percent of Laos's GDP. This sector includes workers such as teachers, health-care workers, and merchants. Compared to more industrial countries, services make up a very small

The beach that serves as the Louangphrabang port on the Mekong River lies at the bottom of a steep hill. People move and stack merchandise from boats and trucks directly on the riverbank. There is no dock.

part of Laos's GDP. This is because so many of its residents live as subsistence farmers in small, remote villages.

One area of the services sector that is growing is tourism. Once closed to foreigners, Laos allows limited stays by travelers. Tourists either fly into Vientiane or travel overland, crossing from Thailand into Laos via the Mittaphab (Friendship) Bridge. The government encourages group tours, which account for the large majority of the nation's visitors.

One of the most popular stops for these tours is the Plain of Jars. Other attractions include the historic capital of Louangphrabang, tribal villages, Buddhist temples, ruins of Khmer cities, and the Pak Ou caves along the Mekong. Visitors to the countryside enjoy Laotian music, local food, and traditional dances and crafts.

## FRIENDSHIP BRIDGE

In April 1994, the Mittaphab Bridge over the Mekong River opened to cars, trucks, and foot traffic. More importantly, it encouraged trade and tourism between Thailand and Laos. Connecting Thailand's Nong Khai and Laos's Vientaine, the Friendship Bridge is 3,800 feet (1,160 m) long. The cost for the bridge was about $30 million. The Australian government paid for most of this, and Australian companies handled the construction. The bridge includes two car lanes and two footpaths. Visitors can also take a shuttle bus between the cities.

Buddha statues fill the lower of the two Pak Ou caves, called Tham Ting. The cave looks out over the Mekong River 50 feet (17 m) below.

Many tourists travel to the eastern edge of Laos for a glimpse of the Ho Chi Minh Trail. Because Laos has no railways and only poor roads, this is a difficult trip. But the hardy traveler can still view rusting Soviet and Chinese trucks along the infamous pathway that saw heavy bombing and fighting during the Vietnam War.

Tourism is helping the Laotian economy by bringing in foreign income. Yet the rising number of visitors is also putting a strain on the country's limited facilities. The government's challenge is to accommodate visitors while maintaining the kind of unspoiled and peaceful setting that most tourists seek.

## Transportation and Communication

A landlocked nation, Laos has a poor transportation system. For example, the road between Vientiane and Louangphrabang often needs

Walking is **the most common form of transportation in Laos.** A woman and child living near Pakxe carry produce from their garden to sell at a small village market.

repair and can become rutted and narrow. During the long rainy season, the monsoons often flood the roads and disrupt traffic. Laos has no railway system and offers little public transportation of any kind between provinces. The Mekong River provides an important route for ferries and cargo boats. But navigation is dangerous during the dry season, when water levels are low. Interior waterways are also hazardous.

About 90 percent of all freight and 95 percent of all passenger traffic in Laos moves by road. Yet the country has less than 6,000 miles (9,660 km) of paved roads, and these are often in poor condition.

In the early 1990s, Laos and Thailand cooperated on the construction of the Mittaphab Bridge. This project, which opened in 1994, fosters a busy trade between the two countries.

Laos has only a few airports, several of which don't even have paved runways. The main airport is in Vientiane. This is where most international travelers enter the country. The nation's state-run airline, Lao Airlines, began operations in 1976 with flights between Vientiane and Louangphrabang. By the 2000s, the airline was flying to airports all over Southeast Asia and into Europe.

Outside its major cities, Laos's communications systems are undeveloped. Even in the cities, many residents don't own a telephone. Cell phone usage has been rising in recent years, especially in the large cities. In the early 2000s, about 300,000 cell phones were registered in Laos. This growth is similar to that of Internet access, which is still mainly available in cities and tourist areas. Internet cafes are increasingly popular as the nation's tourist industry grows.

The government controls broadcasting on Lao National Radio and Lao National Television, though people can also receive channels broadcast from Thailand, China, and other nearby countries.

## Energy

The generation of hydroelectricity has become one of the most important economic activities in Laos. Hydroelectric plants along the nation's rivers produce far more electricity than Laos needs. Laos sells this extra energy to its more industrialized neighbors, such as Thailand, which cannot generate power as cheaply. While the hydroelectric industry offers real growth for the Laotian economy, some people fear that unchecked development will have a harmful effect on the environment. Large dams flood large areas of land and displace thousands of poor residents and wildlife.

Although the Laotian government controls most power producing facilities, the private sector also is involved. Laos is working with companies in Thailand to construct the Nam Theun II Dam, which could cost as much as $1.3 billion to build. Along with Thailand, Australia has helped Laos design and build new hydroelectric projects.

**Water running down steep, mountainous terrain** makes Laos rich in the power that can produce hydroelectricity, one of the nation's largest exports. But this wealth poses environmental challenges too.

Laos does not need a large supply of petroleum because hydro-electricity is readily available. In addition, the country has few gas-fueled vehicles. The country imports most of its gasoline and diesel fuel from Brunei, a small oil-exporting nation on the Southeast Asian island of Borneo. Most Laotian homes use wood charcoal for cooking and heating.

## The Future

Laotians are facing an uncertain future. For the first time in two centuries, the government of Laos is in the position to fully represent itself in the international community. Its progress in this area was highlighted in 2004, when Laos earned Normal Trade Relations status with the United States. This important achievement allows Laos to export goods to the rich markets of the United States. But despite the progress, Laos continues to juggle a variety of economic concerns.

Read the latest news from Laos and learn more about its economy. Go to www.vgsbooks.com for links.

Although foreign governments and citizens are seeking to invest in the country, many Laotians still suffer poverty and malnutrition. Laotian farmers are not always able to feed their families, and the average Laotian worker earns the equivalent of less than one dollar per day. A poorly trained workforce also puts Laos at a disadvantage in the competition for foreign investment. The government needs to prepare workers for new manufacturing and service jobs.

The historic rivalry and prejudice between lowland Laotians and people of the hills is also a continuing concern. The Hmong, for example, were hunted down and killed for their support of U.S. operations and the royalists during the civil war. Many of those who survived the conflict fled the country, and tensions remain high among ethnic groups.

Rapid development and the expanding economy pose other dilemmas for the people of Laos. Although they seek a better way of life, they also fear the loss of their customs, traditions, and beliefs. Controlled development, with a concern for the environment and for maintaining Laotian culture, is the most important challenge to Laos in the twenty-first century.

## Timeline

**CA. 2000 B.C.** The early people of Laos build settlements along the Mekong River.

**A.D. 400s** Indian settlers found Champa. Champasak, the administrative hub, lies along the western bank of the Mekong, near Laos's modern borders with Thailand and Cambodia.

**800s** The Khmer establish Angkor, capital of a powerful Kambuja Empire.

**1100s** The Khmer occupy Vientiane, enslaving many local peoples.

**1253** Kublai Khan destroys Nan Chao, causing a new wave of refugees to move into the fertile land of the Mekong River valley.

**1353** Fa Ngum leads an army and conquers Louangphrabang. The kingdom of Lan Xang is established.

**1373** Fa Ngum's son, Sam Sen Thai, takes over the rule of Lan Xang and begins building Buddhist wats throughout the kingdom.

**1563** The Burmese invade Lan Xang and occupy it for two years.

**1571** The Lan Xang king Setthathirath mysteriously disappears during a battle, leaving the kingdom leaderless.

**1591** Kokeo Koumane becomes the king of Lan Xang.

**1603** Kokeo Koumane reestablishes Lan Xang as an independent state.

**1641** Gerrit van Wuysthoff, an agent of the Dutch East India Company, visits Laos, bringing trade with the West.

**1694** Souligna Vongsa dies, leading to the downfall of Lan Xang.

**1700** Sai Ong Hue, a nephew of Souligna Vongsa, uses a Vietnamese army to capture Vientiane and make Lan Xang a vassal state of Vietnam.

**1805** Siam controls most of modern Laos and chooses Chou Anou to be king of Vientiane.

**1827** Chou Anou leads a failed rebellion against Siam, which takes revenge by destroying Vientiane.

**1860s** The French begin taking control of much of Southeast Asia, which they call French Indochina.

**1893** Vientiane becomes Laos's capital city.

**1899** The French unite the Laotian territories and name Sisavang Vong the country's crown prince.

**1939-1945** During World War II, Japanese soldiers control much of French Indochina, although Laos is spared most of the fighting.

1945    After the war, Prince Phetsarath flees Laos and
        begins an independence movement in Thailand.

1947    The French create a constitution for Laos in hopes it will quiet
        talk of independence.

1949    Prince Souphanouvong, exiled in Vietnam, establishes the Pathet
        Lao, a Communist organization to take over Laos.

1954    Vietnam defeats the French. France recognizes the independence of all
        its Indochina colonies. The Pathet Lao gains control over two northern
        provinces in Laos.

1956    Souvanna Phouma becomes prime minister of the new Laotian government
        without Pathet Lao approval.

1958    Internal struggles cause the Laotian government to collapse.

1960    Bloody civil war begins between the royalists, who favor a capitalist economy
        like those of the West, and the Pathet Lao, who favor Communism. Despite a
        brief cease-fire, the war drags on for thirteen years.

1973    The United States pulls troops out of Vietnam, essentially ensuring Laos's future
        as a Communist state.

1975    The Pathet Lao takes control of Vientiane and sets up the Lao People's Democratic
        Republic (LPDR), making Laos a Communist state.

1986    The Laotian government adopts the New Economic Mechanism, which loosens gov-
        ernment control, allowing private ownership and a more Western-style economy.

1991    The Laotian government approves the country's first constitution since 1975.

1994    The Mittaphab (Friendship) Bridge opens, connecting Vientiane with Thailand. The
        bridge fosters increased trade between the two nations.

1997    The Association of Southeast Asian Nations (ASEAN) admits Laos, a major step
        toward the nation joining the international economy.

1998    Khamtai Siphandon, the former leader of Pathet Lao, becomes the president
        of Laos.

2004    Laos earns Normal Trade Relations status with the United States.

2005    Laos's national soccer team advances to the second round of qualifying
        for the 2006 World Cup.

2006    Choummaly Sayasone replaces Siphandon as President of Laos.
        Laos, along with Thailand, Vietnam, Myanmar, and Cambodia,
        announces plans to step up cooperation in the fight against
        bird flu.

**COUNTRY NAME** Lao People's Democratic Republic (LPDR)

**AREA** 91,430 square miles (236,800 sq. km)

**MAIN LANDFORMS** Annamese Cordillera, Bolovens Plateau, Cammon Plateau, Mekong River floodplains, Tran Ninh Plateau

**HIGHEST POINT** Mount Phou Bia, 9,248 feet (2,819 m) above sea level

**LOWEST POINT** Mekong River, 230 feet (70 m)

**MAJOR RIVERS** Mekong, Nam Ngum, Nam Ou, Nam Tha

**ANIMALS** Asian elephants, butterflies, king cobras, leopards, monkeys, pythons, rock rats, tigers, and wild oxen

**CAPITAL CITY** Vientiane

**OTHER MAJOR CITIES** Savannakhet, Pakxe, Louangphrabang

**OFFICIAL LANGUAGE** Lao

**MONETARY UNIT** Kip. 100 at = 1 kip.

## LAOTIAN CURRENCY

The currency of Laos is called the kip, which can be further divided into 100 *at*. First adopted in 1952, the kip has gone through many changes, especially after the Pathet Lao took control of the country in 1975. The kip is available only in paper notes—Laos has no coins.

Notes are printed in denominations of 1, 5, 10, 20, 50, 100, 500, 1,000, 2,000, 5,000, 10,000, and 20,000 kip.

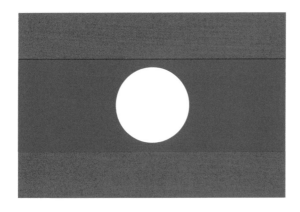

When the Pathet Lao came into power in 1975, it chose a new flag for Laos. The flag has red stripes along the top and bottom, with a wide blue stripe in between them. A large white circle sits in the center of the blue stripe. The flag's red stripes represent the blood shed in the country's long and bloody civil war. The blue stripe represents the Mekong River and the wealth it provides. The white circle symbolizes both the moon over the Mekong and the unity of Laos's people.

The national anthem of Laos is titled "Pheng Xat Lao" (Hymn of the Lao People). Dr. Thongdy Sounthonevichit composed the song in 1941. When the Pathet Lao came into power, the new government kept the tune and wrote new lyrics that proclaim the unity and independence of Laos's people. The anthem ends:

> The Lao people of all origins are equal
> And will no longer allow imperialists and traitors to harm them.
> The entire people will safeguard the independence
> And the freedom of the Lao nation.
> They are resolved to struggle for victory
> In order to lead the nation to prosperity.

 listen to the national anthem of laos. Visit www.vgsbooks.com for a link.

Flag  National Anthem

**OUTHINE BOUNYAVONG** (b. 1942) Bounyavong is a well-known author of contemporary Lao fiction. His writing spans several decades. Born in northwestern Laos, Bounyavong studied briefly in Vientiane. He published his first book, *Sivith Ni Ku Lakone Kom (Life Is Like a Short Play)* at a time when Lao collections were rare. His fiction often comments on Laos's politics and society. Works such as *Death Prince, Dic and Daeng,* and *Mother's Beloved*, all address social issues in Laos, especially the nation's struggle with poverty. Bounyavong uses tales of simple people to illustrate a theme of personal sacrifice for society's benefit. Bounyavong also founded *Vannasin*, a Lao cultural and literary magazine.

**MEE MOUA** (b. 1969) As a Minnesota state senator, Mee Moua holds the highest office of any Hmong American politican. As a senator, she represents a portion of Minnesota's capital city, Saint Paul. Born in the mountains of Laos, Moua fled to Thailand with her family at the end of the Vietnam War. In 1978 she and her family moved to the United States. There she earned an undergraduate degree from Brown University, a master's degree at the University of Texas, and a law degree at the University of Minnesota. She was elected to the senate seat as a Democrat in January 2002 and is an important voice for Minnesota's large Hmong population.

**VANG PAO** (b. 1932) Vang Pao was born in a Hmong village in the mountains of northern Laos. He first became involved in military life during World War II at the age of thirteen. He advanced to the rank of major general in the Royal Lao Army. During the nation's civil war, General Pao allied himself with the United States in opposition to the Pathet Lao. After the Communists seized power in 1975, he left Laos for the United States. Most Hmong consider Pao to be the preeminent leader of the Hmong people in the United States.

**KAYSONE PHOMVIHANE** (1920–1992) Known as the founding father of the Lao revolution, Phomvihane was born in Na Seng, Laos. He attended law school in Vietnam at Hanoi University. But he dropped out to fight the French colonialists as a member of the Vietnamese Association for National Liberation. After returning home, Phomvihane joined the Pathet Lao. In 1955 the Lao People's Revolutionary Party formed, and Phomvihane was selected to be the secretary-general. He served as Laos's prime minister from 1975 to 1991 and president from 1991 to 1992, when he died. In 2005 the town of Chantaburi changed its name to Kaysone Phomvihane City, while Phunkheng Avenue in Vientiane became Kaysone Phomvihane Avenue.

**PHETSARATH RATTANAVONGSA** (1890–1959) Born in Louangphrabang, Rattanavongsa was the son of a high-ranking government official. After attending school abroad, he returned to Laos and worked as a clerk in the office of the French governor in Vientiane. He quickly rose to power, eventually becoming *oupahat* (a rank second only to the king). He created a Lao consultative assembly, reorganized the King's Advisory Council, and set up a system of schools for educating monks in the Pali language. He set up rules to reward, reassign, and promote civil servants. He also created the judicial system, including civil and penal codes.

**PRINCE SETTHATHIRATH** (1534–1572) Setthathirath of Lan Xang is often called one of Laos's greatest leaders. In 1570 he defended his country against the Burmese conquerors, allowing the nation to stay intact. Setthathirath is most famous for building several Buddhist monuments, including the famous Wat Xieng Thong. Two political leaders who had personal grudges against Setthathirath murdered him in 1572. Because he had no grown sons, power struggles soon began, throwing the region into chaos for more than fifty years.

**KHAMTAI SIPHANDON** (b. 1924) Born in Laos's Champasak Province, Siphandon joined the country's revolutionary movement in 1947. He quickly rose through the ranks, becoming chief of staff of the Pathet Lao forces in 1955. When the Pathet Lao came into power in 1975, he became vice prime minister, a position he held for sixteen years. In 1993 he was appointed prime minister. He became president in 1998, a position he held until he stepped down in 2006.

**TIAO SOUPHANOUVONG** (1909–1995) Born in Louangphrabang as a member of the royal family, Souphanouvong went on to become the leader of the Pathet Lao and earned the nickname the Red Prince. He was a well-educated man who spoke eight languages and had a degree in engineering. He used his intelligence to help Pathet Lao take control of Laos in 1975, when he became president. He held that position for eleven years, until he was forced to leave office in 1986.

**KETSANA VILAYLACK** (b. ca 1970) Born in Savannakhet, Laos, Vilaylack is a singer, songwriter, and composer based in Los Angeles, California. After spending her early childhood in Laos, she came to the United States at the age of seven. She quickly discovered a talent for music, which she refined at the Chicago Academy of the Arts. Often called Laos's Madonna, Vilaylack sings in both her native Lao tongue as well as in English. One of her musical goals is to inspire pride in being Laotian. Among her most popular songs is "9/11 Candle of Love," a tribute to the victims of the terrorist attacks of September 11, 2001.

**HLEE XIONG** (b. 1984) Xiong was born in Loei, Thailand, to Laotian parents who had fled the country. The family moved to Akron, Ohio, where Xiong grew up. In 2004 she won the Miss Lao Hmong Pageant in Wisconsin. She has used her crown to help inform people about what happened in Laos during the 1960s and the role that the Hmong played in fighting the Pathet Lao.

**BAN PHANOM** Just a few miles from Louangphrabang, Ban Phanom is a small village showcasing the weaving of silk and cotton textiles on hand looms. The village's market is a good representation of those throughout villages in Laos. In village houses, which also serve as shops, visitors can watch the locals make their crafts.

**HO CHI MINH TRAIL** More and more tourists are traveling to the eastern edge of Laos for a glimpse at what was once the Ho Chi Minh Trail. It's a difficult trip to make, but travelers can still see rusting Soviet and Chinese trucks along the once hidden pathway.

**PAK OU CAVES** A short distance from Louangphrabang, the caves of Pak Ou showcase Buddhist and Lao sculptures carved directly into the limestone walls. The caves may have been used for the worship of the river spirit thousands of years ago, before Buddhism entered the area. Over a span of about six hundred years, about four thousand images were carved into the two caves, called Tham Ting and Tham Phum.

**PLAIN OF JARS** The Plain of Jars provides a glimpse into the ancient past of Laos. Situated in mountainous northeastern Laos, the region of these mysterious stone urns has been open to tourists only since the 1990s. More than three hundred stone jars, believed to be 2,500 to 3,000 years old, are scattered throughout the area.

**SI PHAN DON (FOUR THOUSAND ISLANDS)** The Four Thousand Islands area lies in the Mekong River just above the impassable Khone Falls and north of the Cambodian border. The width of the river at this point allows for hundreds (not thousands, as the name implies) of islands that are home to slow-paced, small villages, temples, and caves. Visitors to these islands enjoy rice fields, coconut trees, colonial houses, waterfalls, and beaches. Don Khong is the largest island, but Don Dhet and Don Khon are more popular among tourists.

**VIENTIANE** Nestled in the Mekong River valley on the border of Thailand, metropolitan Vientiane is the center of Laos's modern culture and commerce. Visitors can enjoy several Buddhist monasteries and temples. Buddha Park, sometimes referred to as Garden of Statues, displays sculptures of Buddha and Hindu gods. The Luang Shrine, a golden relic of the Buddha, is considered the national emblem of Laos. Vientiane visitors can also see National Ethnic Cultural Park, which is home to walking paths, sculptures of Lao literary heroes, and a zoo. This park also offers a beautiful view of the Friendship Bridge.

**WAT XIENG THONG** Although Laos has no shortage of Buddhist temples, many visitors agree that Wat Xieng Thong deserves special mention. Located in Louangphrabang, Wat Xieng Thong sits on a hillside overlooking the Mekong River. Both inside and outside walls are richly decorated, showcasing colorful glassy art.

**animism:** the belief in and worship of spirits. Many people in Laos give offerings to spirits in hopes that the spirits will help them in their earthly lives.

**Buddhism:** a religion dating to the sixth century B.C. that follows the teachings of Siddhartha Gautama, also known as the Buddha

**Communism:** a political and economic model based on the idea of common, rather than private, property. In a Communist system, the government controls most goods and services.

**cordillera:** a group of mountain ranges roughly parallel to one another

**deforestation:** the cutting down of forest land for farming, fuel, or logging

**karst:** limestone formations with sinkholes, underground streams, and caverns

**monarchy:** a government headed by a monarch—usually a king, queen, or royal family member

**monsoon:** a strong wind that blows across the Indian Ocean and southern Asia, often bringing heavy rains

**opium:** an addictive drug made from the dried latex (a milky, white fluid) from the immature seed capsules of the opium poppy

**plateau:** an area of high, flat land

**Prabang:** a golden statue of the Buddha. Said to have magical powers, the Prabang became a symbol of the Laotian state and moved with the royal court whenever it changed locations.

**subsistence farming:** growing and harvesting just enough to feed one's family, without enough left over to sell for profit

**typhoon:** a violent tropical storm

**vassal state:** a nation that pays tribute (a price paid to another nation) to and is partially under the power of that stronger nation

**wat:** a Buddhist temple

Glossary

Selected Bibliography

Anderson, Kym. *Lao Economic Reform and WTO Accession: Implications for Agriculture and Rural Development*. Singapore: Institute of Southeast Asian Studies, 1999.
In this project funded by the United Nations, Anderson details plans to assist the government of Laos in its bid to join the World Trade Organization (an international organization dealing with international trade). The author also includes many charts and tables comparing Laos's economy to the economies of its neighboring countries.

Cable News Network. *CNN.com*. 2006.
http://www.cnn.com (April 13, 2006).
This site provides current events and breaking news about Laos, as well as a searchable archive of older articles.

CIA. *The World Factbook: Laos*. 2005.
http://www.cia.gov/cia/publications/factbook/geos/la.html (January 13, 2006).
This site from the U.S. Central Intelligence Agency offers statistics and background information on Laos's economy, history, demographics, and more.

*Europa World Yearbook, 2005*. Vol. 2. London: Europa Publications, 2005.
Covering Laos's recent history, economy, and government, this annual publication also provides a wealth of statistics on population, employment, trade, and more.

Evans, Grant. *A Short History of Laos: The Land in Between*. Crows Nest, NSW, AU: Allen & Unwin, 2002.
This source covers the history of Laos, from the Lan Xang kingdom through the Pathet Lao takeover and Communist regime, and looks toward future challenges Laos may face.

Nguyen Thi Dieu. *The Mekong River and the Struggle for Indochina: Water, War, and Peace*. Westport, CT: Praeger, 1999.
This book examines both the history and future of the Mekong River and the countries through which it runs.

Prados, John. *The Blood Road: The Ho Chi Minh Trail and the Vietnam War*. New York: Wiley, 1999.
Prados covers the history of the Ho Chi Minh Trail and the Vietnam War.

ReliefWeb. *ReliefWeb: Laos*. 2004.
http://www.reliefweb.int/rw/dbc.nsf/doc104?OpenForm&rc=3&cc=lao (April 13, 2006).
This site presents information on humanitarian concerns in Laos, including food supply, disaster information, and more.

Scott, Joanna C. *Indochina's Refugees: Oral Histories from Laos, Cambodia and Vietnam*. Jefferson, NC: McFarland & Co., 1989.
Twenty-two memoirs of refugees paint a picture of what happened after the Communists took control of much of Southeast Asia in 1975.

Turner, Barry, ed. *The Statesman's Yearbook: The Politics, Cultures, and Economies of the World, 2006.* New York: Macmillan Press, 2006.
This resource provides concise information on Laos's history, climate, government, economy, and culture, including relevant statistics.

"2005 World Population Data Sheet." *Population Reference Bureau (PRB).* 2005.
http://www.prb.org/pdf05/05WorldDataSheet_Eng.pdf (April 13, 2006).
This annual statistics sheet provides a wealth of data on Laos's population; rates of birth, death, fertility, and infant mortality; and other useful demographic information.

U.S. Department of State: Bureau of European and Eurasian Affairs. *Background Notes: Laos.* 2005.
http://www.state.gov/r/pa/ei/bgn/2770.htm (April 13, 2006).
This overview, published annually and regularly updated by the U.S. government, provides an introduction to Laos's government, history, foreign relations, and more.

The World Bank Group. *Lao PDR Data Profile.* 2005.
http://devdata.worldbank.org/external/CPProfile.asp?CCODE=LAO&PTYPE=CP (January 13, 2006).
This World Bank website surveys Laos's economy. The World Bank is an agency offering financial and technical support to developing countries.

*Asia-Pacific*
http://news.bbc.co.uk/1/hi/world/asia-pacific/default.stm
The BBC presents an overview of Asia and the Pacific region, including Laos, with links to breaking news.

Barr, Linda. *Long Road to Freedom: Journey of the Hmong.* Bloomington, MN: Red Brick Learning, 2004.
This book covers the recent history of the Hmong people, including their part in Laos's civil war and their journeys as refugees to the United States.

Behnke, Alison. *China in Pictures.* Minneapolis: Twenty-First Century Books, 2003.
This book gives the history of China, Laos's large neighbor to the north, as well as modern-day news and statistics.

Bramwell, Martyn. *Southern and Eastern Asia.* Minneapolis: Lerner Publications Company, 2000.
This entry in Lerner's The World in Maps series covers Southeast Asia, including Laos.

*Cable News Network (CNN)*
http://www.cnn.com
This site provides current events and breaking news about Laos, as well as a searchable archive of older articles.

Dramer, Kim. *Mekong River.* New York: Franklin Watts, 2001.
Dramer follows the path of the Mekong River through China, Cambodia, Laos, Myanmar, Thailand, and Vietnam, examining its history, geographic features, and environment.

*Encyclopedia of World Geography.* Vol. 2. New York: Marshall Cavendish, 2002.
This source offers detailed geographical facts of all the world's regions, including Southeast Asia. Maps are included.

Jacobsen, Karen. *Laos.* Chicago: Childrens Press, 1991.
Jacobson offers an introduction to Laos, its land, history, and people.

*Laos News*
http://laosnews.net
Laosnews.net provides the latest news out of Laos, Southeast Asia, and around the globe. It includes maps, a factbook, and more.

Levy, Debbie. *The Vietnam War.* Minneapolis: Lerner Publications Company, 2004.
Details the events that led to the Vietnam War, major battles, foreign involvement, and the war's global impact.

Mansfield, Stephen. *Laos.* New York: Marshall Cavendish, 1998.
Mansfield examines the people, geography, religion, and culture of Laos.

Millett, Sandra. *The Hmong of Southeast Asia.* Minneapolis: Lerner Publications Company, 2002.
This book details the lives, culture, and traditions of the Hmong and their homeland.

Further Reading and Websites

**Murphy, Nora. *A Hmong Family*. Minneapolis: Lerner Publications Company, 1997.**
Murphy depicts the history and culture of the Hmong, a unique ethnic group living in Southeast Asia, and describes the experiences of a Hmong family who left Laos to rebuild their lives in the United States. The author includes a Hmong folktale.

*The New York Times on the Web*
http://www.nytimes.com
This online version of the newspaper offers current news stories along with an archive of articles on Laos.

**Taus-Bolstad, Stacy. *Thailand in Pictures*. Minneapolis, Twenty-First Century Books, 2004.**
In this book, readers will find information about Thailand's land, history, government, current events, people, and culture.

**———. *Vietnam in Pictures*. Minneapolis, Twenty-First Century Books, 2004.**
In this book, readers will find information about Vietnam's land, history, government, current events, people, and culture.

*vgsbooks.com*
http://www.vgsbooks.com
Visit vgsbooks.com, the home page of the Visual Geography Series®. You can get linked to all sorts of useful online information, including geographical, historical, demographic, cultural, and economic websites. The vgsbooks.com site is a great resource for late-breaking news and statistics.

**Captions for photos appearing on cover and chapter openers:**

Cover: King Setthathirath built the original Wat Xieng Thong temple in the mid-1500s in Louangphrabang. The flame tree, or tree of life, mosaic on the back wall *(shown here)* is made of colored glass. It was added during a complete remodeling of the temple in the 1960s.

pp. 4–5 Residents of this hilltop village in northern Laos enjoy a sweeping view of mountains from their homes.

pp. 8–9 Farmers plant crops in small terraced fields such as this one throughout mountainous northern Laos.

pp. 40–41 This rural school in Namtha Province has wire mesh windows to allow cool air into the classroom.

pp. 46–47 A Buddhist temple in Louangphrabang houses this beautiful sculpture.

pp. 56–57 Workers on this farm near Louangphrabang harvest rice and tend cattle.

**Photo Acknowledgments**

The images in this book are used with the permission of: © Brian Vikander, pp. 4–5, 13, 52, 61; © XNR Productions, pp. 6, 10; © Cory Langley, pp. 8–9, 18, 46–47, 50, 56–57, 58, 60, 62, 64; © Michele Burgess, pp. 11, 17, 27, 40–41, 43, 51, 54, 68; © Hoang Dinh Nam/AFP/Getty Images, pp. 12, 38, 44, 48; © Reuters/CORBIS, p. 14; © AFP/Getty Images, p. 15; © Pilar Langley, p. 16; © Ken Mclaren/Art Directors, p. 19; © Christopher Liu/ChinaStock, p. 25; © Hulton Archive/Getty Images, pp. 28–29; © Hulton-Deutsch Collection/CORBIS, pp. 30, 35; © Bettmann/CORBIS, p. 32; © Roslan Rahman/AFP/Getty Images, p. 53; © Laura Westlund/Independent Picture Service, p. 69.

Front Cover: © Michael Freeman/CORBIS. Back Cover: NASA.